How a Frog Gets Its Legs

Patricia J. Murphy

Rosen Classroom Books and Materials
New York

Published in 2002 by The Rosen Publishing Group, Inc.
29 East 21st Street, New York, NY 10010

Copyright © 2002 by The Rosen Publishing Group, Inc.

Book Design: Haley Wilson

Photo Credits: Cover, p. 1 © Roger Markham Smith/International Stock;
pp. 2–3, 15, 16 © VCG/FPG International; p. 4 © Zig Leszczynski/Animals
Animals; p. 6 © George Bernard/Animals Animals; p. 8 © National
Geographic/O.S.F./Animals Animals; p. 10 © Tom Lazar/Animals Animals;
p. 12 © Telegraph Colour Library/FPG International; p. 14 © Buddy May/
Corbis.

ISBN: 0-8239-8216-5
6-pack ISBN: 0-8239-8619-5

Manufactured in the United States of America

Contents

Life Begins   5

Eggs to Tadpoles   7

Tadpoles Grow Back Legs   9

Getting Ready to Leave
    the Water   11

Tadpoles Become Frogs   13

Protecting Frogs   14

Glossary   15

Index   16

4

Life Begins

A frog's life begins as a thick, soft, jelly-covered egg in a lake, pond, or **marsh**. Each spring, female frogs and male frogs **mate**. Mother frogs then lay between 200 and 10,000 eggs.

The eggs hatch between three days and three weeks later. Only a few of the eggs live. Fish and other animals eat many of the eggs. Sometimes the pond or stream the eggs are in dries up.

Most mother frogs lay their eggs and then leave them.

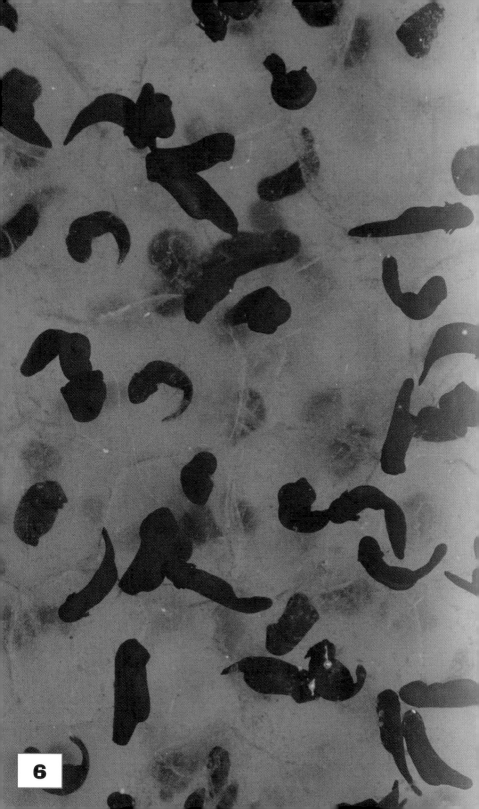

Eggs to Tadpoles

Tiny **tadpoles** wiggle their way out of their eggs. At first, they cannot swim. They have "suckers" on their chins that help them stick to **algae** and twigs. Tadpoles soon grow tails and can swim. They breathe **oxygen** from the water through their **gills**. They eat algae and small fish. Some even eat other tadpoles.

Some tadpoles are so small they are hard to see. Others are almost six inches long.

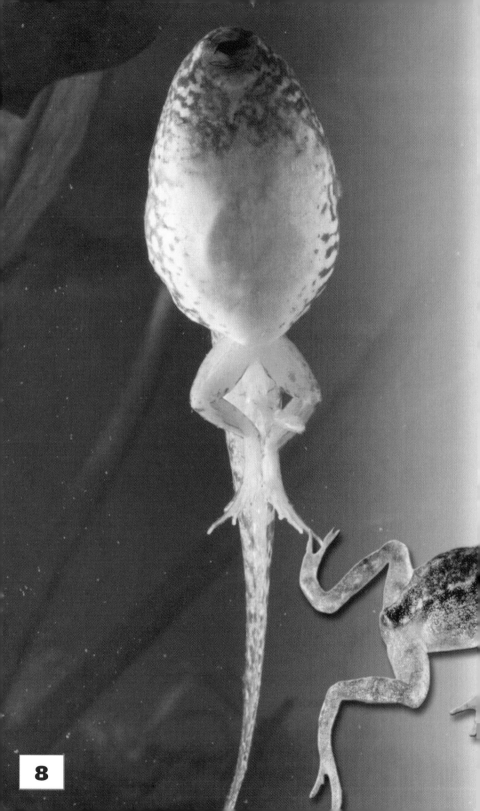

8

Tadpoles Grow Back Legs

Tadpoles grow at different rates.
Some are fully grown in a few weeks.
Others take about three years.

Tadpoles grow back legs first.
They use these legs to help them swim.
Each leg has five long toes. The toes
are **webbed**. The toes act like fins on
fish, helping the tadpoles move through
the water.

Adult frogs use their back legs to jump and dive. The
longest frog jump on record is 33.5 feet!

Getting Ready to Leave the Water

Not long after tadpoles get their back legs, they grow front legs. At about the same time, tadpoles grow lungs to take the place of their gills. Once the lungs form and the gills disappear, tadpoles must lift their heads above water to breathe. Next, the eyes of tadpoles change to allow them to see in water and on land. Finally, tadpoles begin to lose their tails.

A frog's bulging eyes allow it to see in all directions while it watches for insects to eat.

Tadpoles Become Frogs

When their lungs finally finish growing, frogs can live in water and on land. Animals that can live in water and on land are called **amphibians** (am-FIH-bee-anz).

Once on land, most frogs use their **tongues** to catch and eat bugs, worms, and small animals. After they are fully grown, female frogs mate with male frogs—and new life begins again!

There are about 4,000 different kinds of frogs. They live everywhere except Antarctica. It is too cold for them there.

Protecting Frogs

Some people hurt frogs by **destroying** their homes. They **pollute** the lakes, ponds, and marshes where frogs live. They also cut down the forests some frogs call home.

We can help protect frogs by not polluting the water or the air. Can you think of ways to help save the frogs?

Glossary

algae	Tiny plants found in the water of ponds, streams, rivers, and oceans.
amphibian	An animal that can live both in water and on land.
destroy	To damage something so badly that it cannot be used anymore.
gill	A part of a tadpole's body that helps it breathe in water.
marsh	Land that is low, soft, and wet.
mate	When a male and female produce babies.
oxygen	A gas plants give off that people and animals need to breathe.
pollute	To make air, water, or soil harmful to plants and animals.
tadpole	A young frog, usually with just a head and a tail.
tongue	An organ in the mouth used to taste things. Frogs use their sticky tongues to catch food.
webbed	To have skin stretched between the toes to help with swimming.

Index

A

algae, 7

amphibians, 13

E

egg(s), 5, 7

G

gills, 7, 11

L

lake(s), 5, 14

leg(s), 9, 11

lungs, 11, 13

M

marsh(es), 5, 14

mate, 5, 13

P

pollute, 14

pond(s), 5, 14

T

tadpoles, 7, 9, 11

tails, 7, 11

toes, 9

tongues, 13